What Do You Think?

How Much Should Immigration Be Restricted?

Andrew Langley

Heinemann Library
Chicago, Illinois

Customer Service 888-454-2279
Visit our website at www.heinemannraintree.com

Editorial: Andrew Farrow and Rebecca Vickers
Design: Steve Mead and Q2A solutions
Picture Research: Melissa Allison
Production: Alison Parsons

Originated by Chroma Graphics Pte. Ltd.
Printed and bound in China by Leo Paper Group

12 11 10 09 08
10 9 8 7 6 5 4 3 2 1

ISBN: 978-1-4329-0359-6 (hardback)

Library of Congress Cataloging-in-Publication Data
Langley, Andrew.
    How much should immigration be restricted? / Andrew Langley.
        p. cm. -- (What do you think?)
    Includes bibliographical references and index.
    ISBN-13: 978-1-4329-0359-6 (hardback : alk. paper) 1. United
States--Emigration and immigration--Government policy--Juvenile
literature. I. Title.
    JV6483.L36 2008
    325.73--dc22
                                    2007015730

Acknowledgments

The author and publishers are grateful to the following for permission to reproduce copyright material:

©Corbis pp. 29 (epa/Scanpix/Wilhelmsen_Group/Ho-Tampa), 15 (Howard Davies), 26 (Mimi Mollica), 35 (Photo by J. Emilio Flores For The New York Times), 14 (Reuters), 25 (Reuters/Carlos Barria), 47 (Reuters/ Mathieu Belanger); ©Empics p. 39 (PA Photos/PA Archive); ©Getty Images pp. 40, 8 (AFP Photo/Denis Sinyakov), 23 (AFP Photo/Mandel Ngan), p. 45 (Gary Williams), 42 (Joe Raedle); Library of Congress/George Grantham Bain Collection p. 10; Courtesy of Middle School Public Debate Program p. 48; ©2006, Nick Anderson. Distributed by The Washington Post Writers Group. Reprinted with Permission p. 50; ©PA Photos pp. 33, 21 (AP Photo/Gregory Bull), 18 (AP Photo/Jack Kurtz, Pool), 4 (AP Photo/Matt York), 30 (AP Photo/ Rob Griffith); ©Photoedit, Inc. p. 7 (Myrleen Ferguson Cate); ©UPPA pp. 13 (Photoshot), 36 (Photoshot/ Mark Thomas).

Cover photo of border fence reproduced with permission of ©Corbis/Sygma/JP Laffont. Wire frame photo from ©istockphoto.com/angelhell.

The publishers would like to thank Mary Kelly for her comments in the preparation of this title.

Disclaimer

Table of Contents

Some words are printed in bold, **like this**. You can find out what they mean in the glossary.

> *Illegal entry*

A man climbs over a fence at the international border at Nogales, between the United States and Mexico. There are plenty of clues in the picture to show which side is which.

How Much Should Immigration Be Restricted?

Since human history began, people have been on the move. They have traveled in search of food, water, jobs, or wealth. Some have gone short distances—to the next village or town. Others have gone much farther—to a different country or even a different continent.

All of these travelers were **migrants**. They migrated to settle in another place. What is the difference between a migrant and an **immigrant**? If a migrant moves *into* your country or region, he or she is an immigrant. Someone who migrates *out* of your country is called an **emigrant**.

People have been arguing about immigrants for hundreds of years. Sometimes they have blamed the newcomers for causing all kinds of problems, from overcrowding to lack of job opportunities. But at other times they have encouraged immigration because of the economic benefits. The United States, for example, would not have grown into a great nation without the contribution of immigrants.

How much should immigration be restricted? It is a crucial debate in almost every nation in the world, and it will have a key role in shaping the future of society. This book will help you to join in that debate.

How do you know what to think?

This series of books is called *What Do You Think*? The most important words in this question are the last two—"you" and "think." First of all, *you* are the person being asked the question. You are involved, and what matters is your answer to the question. Second, you are being asked to *think*. Your opinion matters, but this does not just mean copying what someone else says. It is your opinion that counts.

Is there a "right" answer?

Suppose somebody asks you, "What is two plus two?" This is a simple question, with just one correct answer: four. If you said "three" or "five," you would be wrong. This is a matter of fact, not opinion.

The title of this book asks a different kind of question: "How much should immigration be restricted?" This is not a simple question, and it does not have one correct answer. You cannot state definitely and finally that immigration is a good or a bad thing. However, you can have an opinion about it.

Everybody has opinions about all kinds of topics. Sometimes they have strong opinions. Immigration is a subject that many people feel very strongly about. It can even make them angry, because they believe that they are right and others are wrong. In extreme cases, this leads to violence and hatred.

How do you form an opinion?

Do you think anger helps people to reach a sensible view on a topic? Does it make their arguments stronger? Or does it get in the way? It is far better to look at a subject calmly and to start out with an open mind. You will be surprised at what you may discover in this way.

You need a lot more than strong feelings if you want to form a worthwhile opinion. The first lesson is to think in a balanced way, so that you can look at all sides of a question before coming to a conclusion. You need to learn how to look for evidence and how to study it. You must also be able to give good reasons for what you believe when you are discussing the subject with others.

The aim of this book is to help you think for yourself and make your own decisions about whether immigration should be controlled. To do this successfully, you need a clear set of steps that will lead you to a balanced and well-informed point of view.

> *What do you think?*
> In debates or discussions with other students, family, or friends, you must be able to back up your opinions with evidence and good reasoning. If you do not do so, your argument will be weak and unsupported.

 Fact or feeling?

An *opinion* is a statement of what someone believes, feels, or judges to be right. It is not a fact, but it can make use of facts.

Reasoning is the process of thinking, understanding, and forming opinions. This must be done logically, considering all possible options.

Evidence is the information (usually facts) we may use to form an opinion.

A *fact* is a statement that we can prove to be true.

> *Keep out!*

Members of a youth movement in Moscow, the capital of Russia, protest against illegal immigrants from countries that were once part of the Soviet Union.

Where is the evidence?

Anyone can have an opinion. You could make a judgment about a subject in a few seconds—just because that is what you feel at the time. But how long will it last? What is the use of having an opinion that does not stand up in an argument? A worthwhile and long-lasting opinion has to be based on evidence. Facts and other evidence give you a firm foundation on which to build your thinking.

Where will you find this evidence? Look for news stories in the papers or on radio and television. Visit your local library and look for books and magazines on the topic. The Internet will contain more facts, figures, case studies, and personal accounts on weblogs (blogs). Search for surveys, opinion polls, government reports, and anything else that gives useful information. Be careful to check these sources, and be aware of any **bias**.

Finally, do not forget that your own experiences could also be valuable. Are you part of a family that recently immigrated? Do you live near one? Is one of your classmates a new arrival in your country? Talk to people around you and listen to the stories they may have to tell.

Listen to both sides of the argument

Do not start out with a set opinion in your head and then try to justify it. People on both sides of the argument will have something valuable to say. Keep an open mind and listen carefully to their views, even if you strongly disagree with them. When examining evidence, look out for a few sources that disagree with your views. You will learn a lot from them.

How much should immigration be restricted? Remember that this kind of question has no definite answer. It is a topic for debate and discussion. All the same, some people believe that an argument is not won by the person who is right, but rather by the person who is best at arguing.

Learn to be a critical thinker

These are the most important steps of all. By thinking critically, you will be able to use your evidence in the most powerful way. First, learn to ask your own questions about the evidence you find. Is it fact, or is it just somebody's idea? Is it honest, or is it biased to one side or the other? Who produced the evidence? Do they have an interest in trying to change your views?

Second, organize your findings. A jumble of facts and figures will only confuse you, so try to build them into a logical argument—think of it as a story, if you like. Do you have similar pieces of evidence that can be put together? Can you place facts side by side so that you can compare and contrast them? What is the best way to make your argument develop from one point to the next?

 Ask yourself ...

Have you formed an opinion?
No? Then ask yourself:
- ✔ What more information do you need to form an opinion?
- ✔ Where would you find that information?

Yes? Then ask yourself:
- ✔ How did you come to form that opinion?
- ✔ On what information did you base your opinion?
- ✔ What was the biggest factor in your decision?
- ✔ Have you ever changed your opinion?

> *Ellis Island*

Between 1892 and 1954, over 12 million immigrants arrived at this island in New York Harbor from all over the world.

What Is An Immigrant?

Are you an immigrant? It is more than likely. Just about everybody in the world today is descended from someone who once moved from one region to another. Scientists believe that human life first developed in central Africa at least 5 million years ago. So, in theory, we could all call ourselves Africans.

From Africa, our ancestors gradually moved out into the rest of the world. They migrated to most parts of Europe and Asia. About 50,000 years ago, humans reached Australia. Much later, the first people crossed into North America and began migrating southward. Very slowly, the world was filling up—with immigrants.

Today, more people are on the move than ever before. There are many reasons for this, from fast transportation systems to the growing misery caused by long-running wars. Immigrants are not just looking for jobs, but also for safety from **oppression**, danger, poverty, and disease.

Many governments now see mass immigration as a big headache and a threat to their countries' prosperity and security. Most have passed laws making it harder for foreigners to cross their borders and become permanent settlers. But is this going to solve the problem? There are now more than six billion humans spread across the world, and the total is rising by an extra million every week. Can a better solution be found?

Mixing and migrating

Where do you live? Where do you come from? These are two very different questions. You may live in the country where you were born. But where were your parents born? Go right back into your family history and you are almost certain to find that some of your roots are in another country.

Ask your classmates if they know their family history. What is their true racial background? It will almost certainly be much more complicated than they think.

Scientists are now using genetics to work out how human beings spread across the world:

The Biggest Family Tree Ever

Ever wondered where your family's ancestors roamed 60,000 years ago?

Now you can find out by participating in the world's most ambitious project tracing the **genetic** and migratory history of the human race.

Members of the general public from all over the world can supply their **DNA** to the Genographic Project, and scientists at The University of Arizona in Tucson will do the genetic analysis. The public DNA sampling is part of a larger undertaking to unravel the origins and migratory history of mankind thousands of years back in time by analyzing genetic samples from at least 200,000 people all over the world.

The project will reveal how our ancestors diversified into different groups and what routes they took as they spread out over the Earth.

[*Medical News Today* 16 Apr 2005, www.medicalnewstoday.com]

Who came from where?

These nations have been shaped by the endless series of migrations that have criss-crossed the world throughout our history.

The United States

In the past 500 years an amazing variety of immigrants has arrived in the United States to join the original Native Americans. Settlers from Europe brought in a **workforce** of slaves, forcibly moving at least ten million Africans to the Americas. After them came vast hordes of people in search of a better life. Most people came from Europe, especially Germany, Great Britain, Ireland,

Italy, Scandinavia, and Russia. Today, the United States is the top destination for people fleeing poverty in Mexico and Central America.

Latin America

After European soldiers conquered most of Latin America in the 1500s, large numbers of Spanish and Portuguese settlers moved in. They searched for mineral wealth and started cattle farms and sugar plantations. During the 1600s, other European settlers established colonies on Caribbean islands.

The United Kingdom

Celts, Romans, Vikings, Anglo-Saxons, and Normans were all immigrants who invaded Britain by 1066 and produced a rich mix of racial backgrounds. Since then, settlers from many more nations have arrived. In the last 50 years, the British population has been joined by large numbers of people from countries such as Pakistan, India, Uganda, and Jamaica as well as from Eastern Europe.

Australia

The aboriginal peoples lived alone in Australia for at least 45,000 years. Then, in 1788 the British founded a colony, which grew rapidly after the discovery of gold. After World War II (1939–45) the Australian government encouraged millions of immigrants from all over Europe to move to Australia.

> *Flying the flag*

Two sisters from London wave Australian flags as they arrive in Sydney Harbour on an immigrant ship in 1949.

Why do people want to migrate?

Throughout history, migration has been an unstoppable force. People want to move, and sometimes nothing can hold them back. What makes them so determined? What are the factors that drive them to travel from one region to another, in spite of the possible danger and hostility?

The push factors

Several things can "push" people out of their own countries. The most powerful of these is fear. War causes death and destruction, and refugees migrate in search of shelter and safety. Since the 1980s, for example, many people have fled from Afghanistan because of invasion, civil war, and cruel governments. Others leave their native lands because they are being persecuted for their religious beliefs or their ethnic background.

Poverty is another big "push" factor. Many countries are poor because of a harsh climate or because of natural disasters, such as earthquakes and floods. These can cause famine, drought, diseases, and other hardships. Employment in poor countries is often hard to find or is badly paid.

The pull factors

There are positive attractions that "pull" migrants toward another country. Many of them are simply opposites of the "push" factors. Refugees from war and **persecution** look for countries that are peaceful and safe. People escaping from poverty go to countries where there are plenty of jobs that are better paid. Many of these immigrants send money from their wages to support their families back home.

Other "pull" factors are less obvious. Students become short-term immigrants in other countries because they have better schools or universities. People from wealthy countries often move to poorer ones that have better climates or lifestyles. People who have committed a serious crime in their own country sometimes run away to another where they know they will be safe from the police.

> **Modern-day Jewish exodus**
>
> During the chaotic and confusing period of the breakup of the former Soviet Union in 1990, many Jews feared persecution and fled to Israel.

What would make you want to change countries?

Most people naturally love the country where they were born and would hate to leave it. Many are also fearful of moving to a foreign land far away where they might be strangers with no friends and no jobs. But sometimes they have little choice.

> *Shelter from bloodshed*
>
> **Refugees from the 1999 civil war in the Serbian province of Kosovo find food and safety at a Red Cross camp in nearby Macedonia.**

Are you proud of your country and your nationality? Can you think of anything that would drive you to leave your friends and family and live somewhere else? Make a list of all the things that would be different. At the top of the list may be the language. Can you speak or understand any foreign languages? Then there is daily life: every society has its own customs and ways of doing things, from eating and drinking to shopping and behaving in public. Would you be brave enough to face these changes?

Masses on the move

Migration throughout the world has increased hugely in the past two centuries. The peak period of mass movement lasted from the 1840s to the 1950s. Why did this happen? The **Industrial Revolution** was changing society and populations were growing fast, especially in Europe. More land and more jobs were desperately needed. There were big, "empty" countries waiting to be filled and vast numbers of people wanting to move.

So, the rush began. By the 1930s, over 60 million immigrants had moved to a new land. About half of these had arrived in the United States from all over the world. The rate has slowed since then, but large numbers of newcomers are still admitted to the United States each year. In the same period, Australia's population has rocketed from a few thousand to more than 20 million—largely thanks to immigration.

How many immigrants are there?

In 2005,
✔ 3 million immigrants became official long-term residents in a different country from where they were born.
✔ altogether, more than 190 million people moved to a different country (most of them for a short term, or illegally); 190 million people is equal to nearly 3 percent of the world's population. This means that 97 percent of the world's population stayed at home.

Speeding up

How did these immigrants reach their goals? Most traveled before the age of aircraft and gasoline engines. They crossed the oceans crammed in sailing ships or steamships. The voyages were often long, dangerous, and uncomfortable, with many migrants having to sleep out on deck. Journeys that once took many weeks now take less than 24 hours in jet aircraft. Add to this the enormous modern network of roads and rail tracks that cross entire continents, and fleets of safer and faster ships on the oceans, and you can see that travel today is much easier and more comfortable than ever before.

Challenges of immigration

So, has immigration become easier? The answer is "yes" and "no." It is easier because of the better transportation systems described above. But it is harder because many countries now make it a lot more difficult for immigrants to gain legal access. In the last 100 years the world has become a much more definite place. Countries have formed themselves into what are called nation states, with their own special laws and cultural identities. They have clear borders, which are guarded and patrolled, and can only be crossed if you have the right kind of passport.

 # The gap between the rich and the poor

With such a large gap between the rich and poor countries, it is not surprising that migrants from poor countries want to leave their homelands. This chart gives you information about some of the richest and poorest countries in the world. GDP means annual "gross domestic product." It is the amount of money a country earns in a year from all of its goods and services. If you divide GDP by the number of people in the population, you can get some idea of the annual income of individuals.

Country	GDP per inhabitant in dollars
Luxembourg	$68,800
United Arab Emirates	$49,700
United States	$43,500
Canada	$35,200
Australia	$32,900
United Kingdom	$31,400
Mexico	$10,600
Pakistan	$2,600
Haiti	$1,800
Ethiopia	$1,000
Zambia	$1,000
Afghanistan	$800
Somalia	$600

> *Presidential visit*

U.S. President George W. Bush talks to patrol
commanders on a visit to the Mexico border in 2006.

Immigration— Is It Good Or Bad For A Country?

Many people support the call for restricting the number of immigrants who can enter a country. Some go even further and argue that immigration should be stopped altogether. Why? They believe that immigration is a bad thing and harms a nation's **economy**, culture, and society. Other people say there should be few restrictions. In their opinion, immigration is a good thing for a country. It boosts the economy and brings variety and freshness.

This book will help you decide which viewpoint you support. But first you have to examine an important question. Are all immigrants the same, and do they deserve the same treatment? It is important to understand that there are two kinds of immigrant—legal and illegal. Today, most national governments have strict controls regarding immigration. They allow only a fixed number of people to settle in their country. Other foreigners are permitted to enter the country for a temporary stay. These are the "legal" immigrants.

However, there are many thousands (maybe millions) more who are desperate to move to another country. They cannot get official permission to immigrate, but they travel anyway. These people enter a country in a variety of ways—hidden from official eyes. They are "illegal" immigrants. Should they be stopped? Can they be stopped?

Crossing the border: The United States and Mexico

The land border between Mexico and the United States stretches for 1,950 miles (3,140 kilometers). Much of it is harsh desert. About 350 million people cross this border every year—legally. But another million (mostly Mexicans) cross it illegally. The U.S. government puts a large amount of money into guarding this border with soldiers, fences, **radar**, video systems, and "spy in the sky" aircraft.

Is it worth it? Do controls work? Ask yourself:

• Why do so many Mexicans risk their lives to reach the United States?
• What are the other dangers for illegal immigrants in the border area?
• Why should the U.S. government spend millions of dollars trying to stop them?
• Do you believe all the information given by both sides?

Look at this article and for other evidence to help you answer these questions.

President Bush's Plan to Stem Tide of Illegal Immigrants

Bush is seeking money from Congress for the deployment of up to 6,000 National Guard troops to help Border Patrol agents.

"They will operate **surveillance** systems, build **infrastructure**, analyze intelligence, and provide training," Bush said.

Bush said that since he took office in 2001 the number of border agents has increased from 9,000 to nearly 12,000. New fencing, lighting, and cameras have been added in key locations.

"We're in the process of making the border the most technologically advanced in the world," Bush said. Opponents contend the barriers would shift illegal immigrant and smuggling traffic to areas of the border without fencing.

More than 85 percent of the illegal immigrants come from Mexico, and most are sent home within 24 hours.

[Source: CNN report, May 18, 2006]

> *Caught in the act*

U.S. Border Patrol agents detain three illegal immigrants near the Mexican border at Fasabe, Arizona, in 2006. An astounding 1.1 million illegal immigrants were arrested along the U.S.—Mexico border in 2006.

 Illegal immigration slang

Various slang terms have come into use for people smugglers and illegal immigration:

Coyote Someone paid to smuggle illegal immigrants across the Mexican border into the United States

Corridor of Death Part of the Sonoran Desert that runs from the Mexican state of Sonora into Arizona. Hundreds of migrants die every year trying to cross into the United States by this route. They can fall prey to dangerous bandit gangs as well as the extreme heat and difficult terrain.

General Person who organizes immigrant groups and gets them into freight railroad cars

Snakehead Someone who smuggles people from China into the United States or Western Europe

For restricting illegal immigration

"The ongoing migration of persons to the United States in **violation** of our laws is a serious national problem **detrimental** to the interests of the United States."
Ronald Reagan, former U.S. president

"I'm deeply sympathetic to the huge numbers of people looking to come here today to escape suffering and poverty in their own lands. But as a country, we cannot afford to have a total open-door policy without any restrictions on entry."
Ed Koch, former mayor of New York City

"They'll flood our schools. Our health-care system will collapse, and our social service system will end up being overtaxed. We've got to get control of our borders, because if we don't, we're going to see our economy collapse."
James Sensenbrenner, member of the U.S. House of Representatives

Are illegal immigrants bad for the United States?

There is no doubt that illegal immigration makes a big impact on the United States. Large numbers of foreign nationals enter the country and settle there every year. Does this nonstop flow of newcomers damage U.S. society? Many people think so. They say illegal or uncontrolled immigrants will

* take jobs from native-born Americans. (There are only so many jobs to go around. If immigrants take them, it means more American nationals will be unemployed.)
* accept lower pay than non-immigrants. (This means that pay will be lower for everybody.)
* overburden the welfare system. (Huge numbers of poor immigrants claim welfare, education, and health benefits from the government. This means that U.S. citizens have to pay higher taxes to finance the extra demand.)
* change the country's national identity. (Foreigners bring their own habits and customs with them, including different languages, foods, clothes, and religious beliefs. These are bound to have an effect on American culture.)
* increase the risk of terrorist attacks. (Religious **fundamentalists** and other extremists could enter the United States, and then plan deadly strikes.)

Looking at the evidence

Is this all true? What evidence can you find that would make you agree or disagree with these claims? Look for facts about employment and pay levels

Anti-illegal immigration protesters demonstrate on Capitol Hill, Washington, D.C., demanding tougher border controls and a crackdown on illegal immigrants.

throughout the nation and for **statistics** about welfare claimants. Read about the lifestyles of some of the most recent legal immigrants to the United States, such as Vietnamese and Afghan people. Think about national security.

Ask yourself: Why do some people object so strongly to immigration? Obviously, many arguments can be backed up with facts and figures, particularly about illegal immigration. But is there something more?

All throughout history, people have been alarmed by foreigners. This feeling is called "xenophobia" (a Greek word meaning "fear of strangers"). Many people in the world today believe that their countries belong to people who were born there. In their view immigrants, legal or illegal, simply do not belong.

 Taking jobs from others?

The number of Mexican immigrants in the whole U.S. labor market is approximately 3.5 percent. The proportion of Mexican immigrants in the U.S. industrial workforce by occupation is as follows:

Agriculture and forestry	15.5 percent
Construction	8.5 percent
Manufacturing	7.0 percent
Mining	3.0 percent
Transportation and warehousing	2.5 percent

(Figures taken from most recent U.S. census information)

Benefits of immigration

"Everywhere immigrants have enriched and strengthened the fabric of American life."
John F. Kennedy, former U.S. president

"Remember, remember always, that all of us . . . are descended from immigrants and revolutionists."
Franklin D. Roosevelt, former U.S. president

"The high-tech world we are now dominating is dependent on educated folks, but we're short of workers. It is to our nation's advantage to encourage high-powered, smart people to come into our country."
George W. Bush, U.S. president

"Legal immigrants have long come to America seeking a fair chance to contribute and, in the process, have enriched our culture and strengthened the nation. Immigrants have always pulled their weight."
George Soros, financier and philanthropist

"It's thanks to us that this country is what it is to this day, and what it will be for the future."
Ardaya Barron, Bolivian immigrant

Is immigration good for the United States?

Most immigrants move to the United States to find a better quality of life. They look for the benefits of living in a wealthy, powerful, and developed nation. But do immigrants bring benefits to U.S. life? Supporters of increased immigration say that legal newcomers:

- actually make the United States wealthier. (Economists estimate that immigrants add $20 billion a year to the economy—that is, about $80 for each U.S.-born resident.)
- allow many companies to profit from cheap labor costs. (This means that they can sell their goods cheaper, so consumers also profit.)
- enrich U.S. society by bringing in fresh cultural influences. (The United States is already an exciting mixture of world cultures.)
- strengthen the workforce. (Immigrants tend to take the "dirtier" jobs, such as cleaning and fruit picking, that Americans are reluctant to do. Without immigrant labor, there would be employment shortages in these areas.).

> *New Americans*

A group of 250 legal immigrants takes the oath of loyalty to the United States during a citizenship ceremony in Miami, Florida.

 New life in the new world

The Statue of Liberty in New York Harbor is a symbol of freedom and a new beginning. It was the first thing many immigrants saw as they neared the United States. In 1883 Emma Lazarus wrote a poem in which the statue speaks:

"Give me your tired, your poor,
Your huddled masses, yearning to breathe free,
The wretched refuse of your teeming shore.
Send these, the homeless, tempest-tost to me:
I lift my lamp beside the golden door."

A century later, have Americans changed their minds?

> *Searching for safety*

Over 300 migrants from Eritrea, East Africa, are crammed into this small boat. It was spotted by Italian coastguards in the Mediterranean Sea and brought to safety.

Should We Shelter People Who Are In Danger?

So far, this book has looked at the practical side of the debate about immigration. This can include the threat to jobs and welfare, the dangers of overcrowded housing in cities, and the effects of foreign cultures.

But the immigration argument also has a moral side. This includes questions about how we should behave toward other inhabitants of the world. Is it right or wrong to restrict the number of foreigners who can enter our country? Shouldn't we welcome people who are searching for safety and an escape from poverty and fear?

After all, those who live in the wealthy and developed nations of the world are very lucky. Most of them enjoy a high standard of living—enough to eat, good medical services, and protection from violence. They also enjoy many kinds of freedom—freedom to elect their own leaders, to express their own opinions, and to follow their chosen religious faith.

For many people, however, the world is a harsh and frightening place. Poverty, war, **repression**, and natural disaster can make life unbearably hard. It is not surprising if large numbers want to give themselves a better chance by finding a new home elsewhere. This is exactly what migrants have done all through human history. Does anyone have the moral right to stop them? Should they not be given the chances your ancestors had?

The Tampa case

On August 26, 2001, a fishing boat from Indonesia was drifting helplessly in the Indian Ocean. It was crammed with 438 refugees who had fled from Afghanistan. The Norwegian cargo ship *Tampa* came to their rescue and took them aboard.

The *Tampa*'s captain decided to take them back to Indonesia. But the refugees wanted to go to Australia. They said they would all jump overboard rather than go back. The captain agreed to drop them at Christmas Island, part of Australian territory.

But the story turned nasty. The Australian government did not want the refugees and told the *Tampa* to keep out of its waters. Soldiers boarded the ship and found many of the refugees were badly sick. In the end, the Afghans were loaded onto another vessel and taken to **detention camps** on the Pacific island of Nauru.

What happened next

The incident caused a scandal in Australia and around the world. It highlighted the two sides of the immigration debate. Was the Australian government being selfish and avoiding its human rights duties? Or was it showing a strong and determined attitude toward illegal immigrants? There were supporters on both sides.

Over the following months, the 438 Afghans from the *Tampa* were joined in the camps by hundreds of other illegal immigrants. They were part of a wave of Asian people who made the dangerous journey looking for "asylum," or refuge, in Australia. Some were eventually allowed to settle in New Zealand, while others were kept imprisoned on Nauru for several years.

Why keep them out? What some Australian politicians said …

✔ The asylum seekers were simply "line-jumpers," falsely claiming to be refugees in order to gain illegal entry into the country—ahead of those who had applied in the proper way.

✔ If Australia accepted these boat people, the floodgates might open. "People smugglers" would see Australia as a soft target and bring in many more illegal immigrants.

✔ The group of Afghans might contain terrorists in disguise.

> *Without a home*

Some of the rescued refugees camp out beneath the towering stacks of cargo containers on board the *Tampa* in the Indian Ocean in August 2001.

 ## Captain under pressure

The captain of the *Tampa* was Norwegian Arne Rinnan. He was put in a very difficult position. On the one hand, his new refugee passengers were unwilling to be disembarked in Indonesia, to the point where they would rather lose their own lives. On the other hand, he had the Australian government saying his ship could not enter its waters. All he could do was sit tight and wait. Rinnan told a reporter at the time: "If we move, they say they will go crazy, and threaten with jumping ship, so for the safety of everybody I stay put."

The Australian government was not happy with Rinnan's stance. It listened in to his phone conversations from the ship and eventually sent in its army to clear off the refugees on to Christmas Island. Others around the world saw his actions as wise and humane. He was knighted by the king of Norway for his bravery and humanitarian values. In the time since the *Tampa* crisis, Captain Rinnan has been named Shipmaster of the Year by the Nautical Institute and also by Lloyds List (the world's leading shipping information service). Commenting on his actions, the Norwegian Shipowners' Association said, "To us it is self evident that people in distress are rescued regardless of who they are and where they come from."

Why did they leave their homeland?

Why did the Afghans set out in an overcrowded and leaky boat to cross a vast area of perilous ocean? They had paid a lot of money for the voyage and put their lives in great danger. What drove them to do it?

The 438 travelers were refugees (people seeking a refuge from danger). They had left their homeland because they believed their lives were under threat. Their country, Afghanistan, had been ruled since the late 1990s by a hardline group called the **Taliban**. The Taliban persecuted anyone who disagreed with them, imprisoning, killing, and maiming their victims and imposing harsh laws. Ordinary life became a nightmare for many Afghan people, and large numbers decided to emigrate.

> Let them go!

People who disagreed with the Australian government detaining refugees on Nauru protested on the streets of Sydney in 2005, halting rush-hour traffic.

How many refugees?

The United Nations High Commissioner for Refugees (UNHCR) is an agency of the United Nations Organization, which works for the welfare of refugees throughout the world. Here are some of the most recent UNHCR statistics (2004):

Refugees who are homeless, but still in their country of origin	8 million
Refugees in camps near the borders of their country of origin	10 million
Refugees who are seeking asylum overseas	1 million
Others	3 million
Total number of refugees worldwide	22 million

Should refugees get special treatment?

The 438 travelers rescued by the *Tampa* were refugees. But were they a special case? Did they deserve different treatment from other immigrants trying to become citizens in Australia? After all, most of the world's refugees do not go far. They stay in or close to their own country, hoping that one day they will be able to go home.

Were the *Tampa* refugees different from other illegal immigrants? They did not move across the world in search of better job prospects, better education, or better housing. They left their homeland because they feared for their lives. Do you think the Australian government should have allowed them in immediately?

What are asylum seekers?

Asylum seekers are a special type of refugee. They travel to another country to claim "asylum"—a safe place where they will be protected from arrest or persecution by their own government. They have to apply for asylum status and may have to show that they would be in danger of their lives if they were forced to return home.

Is it easy to be accepted for asylum? The process can take a very long time. Meanwhile, the asylum seekers often have to live in detention camps (like the *Tampa* refugees) for months or even years. This can be a distressing time. The conditions in the camps are sometimes appalling, with a lack of proper food, water, and medicines, and with families being split up. Some refugees go on hunger strike in protest of their harsh treatment.

Downfall of a people smuggler

What sort of people take money to smuggle refugees illegally into another country? These people are certainly breaking the law. Here is the story of what happened to one of them when she was finally arrested and tried in court. There are many people smugglers all over the world who become wealthy through this trade in humans. Why do you think anyone would pay to become an illegal immigrant?

Mother of All "Snakeheads" Gets 35 Years in Jail

Cheng Chui Ping, infamous as the "Mother of all Snakeheads," had been operating a thriving people smuggling operation from China's notorious Fujian coast since 1991.

Ping aka "Big Sister Ping" was bringing in large numbers of illegal immigrants to North America.

Recently, Cheng, 57, who ran her operations out of New York's Chinatown, was sent to jail for 35 years.

U.S. authorities said her jailing puts one of the world's most prolific human traffickers—or "snakeheads"—behind bars.

She was primarily convicted for organizing the voyage of the Golden Venture, which had about 300 Chinese immigrants on board when it ran aground off New York in 1993. Ten of them died after being pitched into the sea.

Prosecutors said the woman ran a multimillion-dollar ring using the violent Fuk Ching Chinese street gang that crammed immigrants into planes, cars, and trucks with fake floors and ships with dungeon-like conditions where one bathroom served hundreds of people.

[Source: Mata Press Service (*Asian Pacific Post*, www.asianpacificpost.com), March 27, 2006]

Questions to ask yourself

- Should people like Cheng Chui Ping be seen as criminals? They claim they are helping immigrants on their quest to find a new and better life.
- Why do people have to hide in places with "dungeon-like conditions"? Many illegal immigrants have died of suffocation during their journeys.
- What sort of travel documents do refugees need before they are legally allowed to enter another country? What do you need when you visit abroad?
- How many "people-smugglers" or "human traffickers" are there around the world? They certainly operate in many countries, though nobody knows how many illegal immigrants they transport.
- Would there be fewer refugees in foreign countries if there were no people-smugglers? Crossing a border illegally would be much more difficult.
- Is there a difference between a "people-smuggler" and a "human trafficker"? See what evidence you can find.

 Price of a new life

How much do illegal immigrants pay to be smuggled into another country? In 2005 the average price for one person to be transported from Asia into the United States was estimated to be $60,000.

> See-through smuggling

This image was taken by an X-ray machine and shows people hidden inside a truck. Machines like this are used at many ports.

Who is to blame?

What makes refugees run away from the country where they were born? There are many answers, as this book has shown. Among the most important of them is fear. People flee from civil war, invasion, tyranny, and all other human-made disasters that create brutality and violence.

So, can we blame the people who start wars and rule by terror? Without these horrible things, there would certainly be fewer asylum seekers and innocent displaced refugees. Afghanistan, for example, has suffered from two major invasions, a long and bitter civil war, and a repressive regime within the last 30 years. Millions of Afghans have emigrated. If the violence had not occurred, they would have stayed at home.

There are plenty of others who could be blamed for increasing the flood of refugees and other immigrants to the developed countries of the world. What about the people who make a profit from illegal immigrants? The smugglers have grown rich—and the more migrants they move, the more money they make. The "**gangmasters**" and other businesspeople who employ the foreigners have also become wealthy because they can pay very low wages. Their illegal workers are in no position to argue.

Fleeing the bloodbath of war

The United Nations High Commissioner for Refugees (UNHCR) calculates that 12 percent of all Iraqis have fled their homes since the 2003 U.S.-led invasion. Where are most of them now?

Inside Iraq, but displaced	1.7 million
In Syria	1 million
In Jordan	700,000
In Egypt	80,000
In Lebanon	40,000
(Figures for January 2007)	

What happens to asylum seekers in the United States?

About 100,000 asylum seekers arrive in the United States each year to apply for refugee status. But being accepted for asylum is a long and nerve-wracking process. Refugees have to claim asylum in the country, either by voice or in writing. Officials interview them and decide whether they deserve to stay and go on to the next step. Many are swiftly rejected and sent back to their homelands. The rest are examined again and then placed in detention camps. The U.S. government holds about 3,000 asylum seekers in camps. These are often in remote areas with poor facilities. Some are just county jails, where the refugees mix with ordinary criminals.

Asylum seekers may have to stay in these camps for anything from a few months to three years before the government grants their claim. They also have to pass a language test to make sure they are fluent in English. They may then have to wait for another six months before they can apply for a work permit.

A harsh deterrent

Why is the asylum procedure so complicated? Why is the detention policy so harsh? Speaking of asylum seekers arriving by sea, a U.S. spokesperson answered that the policy is harsh "in order to deter others from taking the life-threatening boat trip and [to] ensure our **maritime** defense assets are not diverted from their national security mission."
U.S. Immigration, Customs, and Enforcement (ICE)

> *Stopped at the border*
Mothers and children who have entered the United States illegally wait in a detention center in Nogales, Arizona, after being arrested by border guards. About 27,000 illegal immigrants are in U.S. detention centers every night.

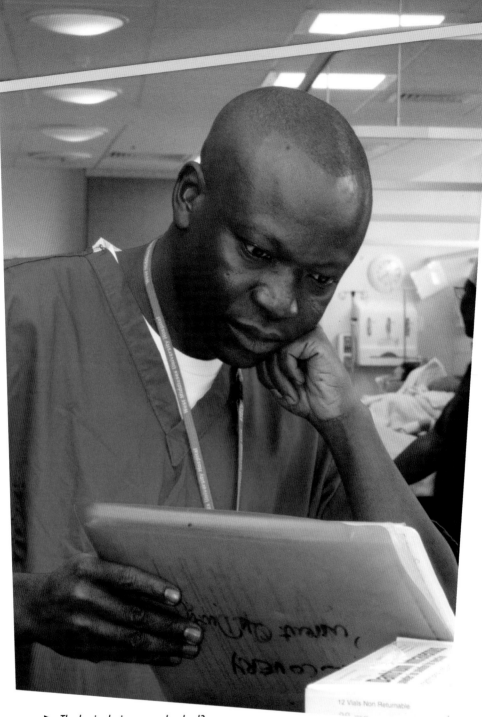

> *The brain drain—good or bad?*

Hospitals in developed countries are better equipped, and pay and working conditions are better.

The Brain Drain

What is the most important issue in the immigration debate? Many people would say that it was the impact of immigrants on their new country, particularly illegal immigrants. Some call the impact damaging, while others call it beneficial. In any case, the focus of attention is usually on the destination of the migrants.

There is another side to the argument, which is often forgotten. What happens to the country that is left behind? What effect does the disappearance of part of the population have on the people who remain? In some cases, it might bring advantages—less overcrowding and less competition for jobs and resources. Workers overseas often benefit their native countries by sending home regular sums of money.

However, there is also a crucial downside. A significant number of migrants come from the educated **professional** classes. Doctors, nurses, teachers, and engineers are attracted to other countries because they will get better pay, conditions, and opportunities. Few ever return to their homelands. This kind of emigration is called "the brain drain." The loss of intelligent, talented, and highly trained people is a serious blow to any country. Statistics show that it hits small and developing countries the hardest, because they can least afford to lose a valuable part of the workforce. Where do these "brains" end up? The majority migrate to wealthy, developed regions, such as the United States, Australia, and the European Union.

The Ever Grim Story of Brain Drain

A report from the World Health Organization (WHO) says that in Africa alone, where health needs and problems are greatest, around 23,000 qualified **academic** professionals emigrate annually to Europe and the Americas in search of better life opportunities.

Roughly 50 percent of the total population of doctors in Ghana are practicing in the U.S. alone; while between 70 and 100 doctors emigrate from South Africa every year. Nigeria alone loses more health workers than other African countries combined. Some estimates put the number of Nigerians outside at one out of every ten black doctors in the U.S.

The migration is already causing havoc to the country and the growth of its health care system. There has been a reduction in the number of newly registered doctors from 1,750 in the year 2000 to 800 in 2002, a 60 percent reduction.

The migration is a major health disaster in most African nations. For instance, it is alarming and pathetic that Malawi, a small, poor African country, has more of its doctors practicing in Manchester, England, than in all of Malawi.

According to the WHO report, a typical Nigerian health professional in the U.S. contributes about $150,000 per year to the U.S. economy.

[Source: *The Guardian*, May 5, 2005]

Who loses the most?

This WHO report concentrates on how the "brain drain" affects one continent—Africa. Do you find the quoted figures shocking? What are these nations losing besides their skilled professionals? Most of them have schools and colleges that give a good education. If the best qualified students emigrate, then that education, and the investment behind it, will be lost to another country.

Why are African countries so vulnerable? Look for evidence about the economic conditions in the places that are mentioned in the extract. You will see that most of them suffer from widespread poverty, which is partly caused by natural disasters such as drought and contagious disease. These can lead to other social problems, including high crime rates and industries that fail due to lack of money.

The brain drain worldwide

Is Africa the worst hit? There are many other developing countries throughout the world—especially in Asia and Central and South America. Many doctors, teachers, and other trained men and women leave these places, too, seeking better opportunities in wealthier lands. Do they suffer as badly as Nigeria and Malawi?

The larger countries seem to feel the effects of the brain drain less severely. Nations such as India, Brazil, and China lose just as many professionals to emigration. But because they have big populations, the loss does not seem so great. Countries with small populations, such as Haiti or Jamaica, are much more badly harmed. Nearly 80 percent of people who get college degrees there end up working abroad.

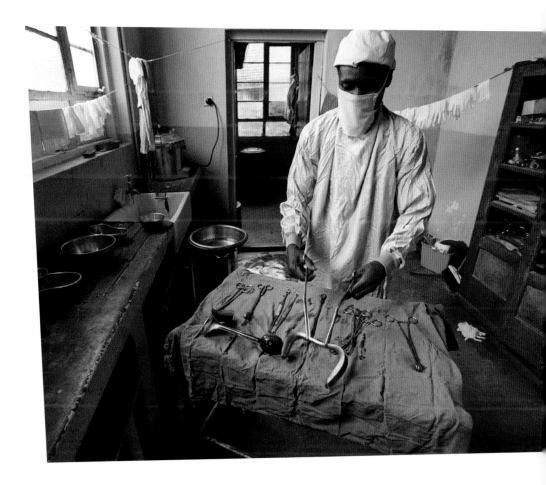

> Difficult conditions

This surgeon in Tanzania is preparing his operating room for a patient. The conditions in a modern, Western hospital would make his job much easier.

Why do so many professionals emigrate?

The direction of the brain drain is usually the same: from the poorer, developing countries to the rich countries. So, the reasons why highly educated people want to move are much the same as other migrants. They are looking for better pay, better living conditions, and better opportunities to be successful. Many are also fleeing violence, corruption, or instability in their countries of origin.

But do some "brain drainers" have special reasons to go abroad? People who have gone through a long and hard period of training should be highly valued members of society. They expect to be well paid. They also expect to work in places (such as hospitals and science laboratories) that are properly equipped

> *Modern facilities*

Not all hospitals in Africa are under-staffed and under-resourced. This modern, well-equipped hospital in Namibia is where Angelina Jolie and Brad Pitt's daughter was born.

The brain drain: What do they think?

"When I was 18 years old, the political and social environment in Argentina, my native country, was desperate and offered very little to young people who wanted to work and study. Many of us felt that we had no opportunities at all and were very frustrated. Since I had an uncle and aunt who lived in the U.S., they offered that I could stay with them if I came." *Oscar, who immigrated from Argentina to the United States as a young man*

"I feel guilty when I visit hospitals in Zambia. I work at an English hospital with many qualified anesthesiologists on the staff. In the whole of Zambia, there is only one! The medical schools train them, but they all leave when they are qualified." *Farzin, an anesthesiologist in the United Kingdom*

"My parents were eager to get us the best education possible in circumstances where we were safe from violence. It's what any parent would want for their children." *Elaine, a bank manager in the United States who left Zaire (now the Democratic Republic of the Congo) as a teenager with most of her family*

and up-to-date. If they cannot find these at home, they will not be able to work at their best—so they leave.

No drain—no gain

Who stands to gain most from the brain drain? Obviously, the new host countries benefit from the arrival of highly trained specialists like doctors and scientists. They bring important skills and intelligence, which every society needs. They also take away skills and intelligence from their homelands.

But is this always a major loss? Sometimes the emigrants are replaced by new immigrants. For instance, in recent years large numbers of Canadian professionals have moved to work in the United States. This obviously leaves an important gap in Canada's workforce. But the gap has been filled by skilled immigrants arriving in Canada from other countries. This process has been called the "brain exchange."

> *Passport control*

A U.S. customs and border protection officer checks the passport of a new arrival at Miami International Airport in Florida.

What Has To Change?

Most of this book has been about the issues involved with controlling immigration. It has examined questions on both sides of the debate, using stories and statistics from the recent past.

Have you reached an opinion yet? You may have decided that too much immigration is harmful to a country, and that it should be curbed by tougher new laws. Or maybe you believe that immigration brings huge benefits and should not be restricted at all. Perhaps the best answer lies somewhere in between. One thing is certain. Immigration is having an enormous effect on our world. It can change societies and cause huge upheavals in the economy.

Clearly, the flow of people from one country to another is almost impossible to stop. But what can we do to change the present chaos? Can we continue to allow legal immigrants (and even more illegal ones) to arrive in such huge numbers? If we decide to restrict immigration still further, what sorts of measures are needed? Will they work?

Whether you are for or against more restrictions on immigration, it is clear the present system is not working well. It is not successful at keeping out illegal immigrants or even at keeping count of them. For legal arrivals, the entry process is often long and complicated. All this must be improved before the many problems over immigration can be solved.

Should there be stricter controls?

Would better controls make immigration easier? Some people argue that stricter laws and tougher barriers will stop illegal immigrants from entering a country. Dry up the flow of unwanted foreigners, and there will be more money and time to spare for welcoming legal newcomers. This will make the processing of applications much quicker and easier.

Where should these new controls be targeted? Many immigrants enter a country through airports and seaports, where they can be easily spotted and identified. But many more cross land borders that are unguarded or they land from boats on remote parts of the coast. These are the areas that are the most difficult to patrol.

What methods can be used?

Passports have been around for hundreds of years and were the first way of restricting immigration. A passport is proof of people's nationality and allows them to leave and return to their own country.

Now technology is providing many new and more accurate ways of checking someone's identity. Electronic systems can record a fingerprint, the **retina** of an eye, and even the pattern of a voice—all of these things are different for each of us. Thanks to modern science, there are also dozens of new ways of keeping watch on land borders. Very accurate long-range cameras are mounted on tall towers or carried in unmanned "**drone**" aircraft. Electronic **sensors** detect heat from bodies or vibrations in the ground. Steel fences can be topped with razor wire or electrified. How effective will these new methods be?

The barrier billions

Here are U.S. government estimates for a barrier to run along the 2,000-mile (3,219-kilometer) Mexico border from the Gulf of Mexico to the Pacific:

10-feet- (3-meter-) high wire fence topped with razor wire
$851 million

The same fence, electrified
$1.2 billion

12-feet- (3.6-meter-) high, 2-feet- (0.3-meter-) thick concrete wall
$2 billion

Double steel and wire fence with 100-yard (91-meter) gap, lights, and sensors
$8 billion

Border barriers: Do they work?

Here is a 2007 story from the website of Minuteman, a border watch organization that campaigns for a barrier along the U.S.–Mexico border.

Minuteman Fence Rising on Border Ranch

The Minuteman Civil Defense Corps has financed and coordinated the construction of a 0.9-mile-long, 13-foot-high steel mesh fence east of Naco, Arizona. So far, about a quarter mile is finished. Although the barrier covers only a tiny section of the 362 miles of international border in Arizona, the Minuteman organization insists the impact on illegal immigration will be more than just symbolic. It will "let the government know that it's not as difficult to secure the borders as they lead us to believe." The barrier is expected to cost about $650,000.

> Block them out!

Workers fix metal mesh to high steel beams in the Arizona desert. This mile-long fence on the border between Arizona and Mexico has been paid for by an American anti-illegal immigration group, to show what can be done to close the border.

Should migrants be free to go anywhere they want?

Some people say there should be no restrictions at all on immigration. Everyone should be free to live and work wherever they like. This is called "open immigration." There are many opponents of this view.

Campaigners have two main arguments in favor of open immigration. First, they believe that rich countries should welcome migrants from poor countries and let them enjoy higher living standards. Keeping them out is simply being selfish. The second argument is practical. They say that the world should be a free marketplace, and that people should be allowed to go where there are jobs. The result will be a more balanced economic system throughout the world.

What would happen if immigration were totally unrestricted?

Nobody really knows what would happen if immigration were totally unrestricted. No country in recent history has ever lifted all restrictions on the entry of foreigners. For many decades, the United States had an almost open policy on new settlers (although it was limited mainly to Europeans). This policy ended with the Immigration Act of 1924, which introduced much stricter laws.

However, a few countries have recently made immigration much easier for some people. In Europe, for example, the 27 states of the European Union (the EU) passed a law giving freedom of movement to people who live there. Citizens of the member countries are free to move to another member country. They can live, work, and even vote there without restrictions. This freedom has led to a huge migration of workers from poorer countries (such as Poland and Bulgaria) to richer ones.

 The most open country?

Canada has the highest immigration rate in the world. It admits more immigrants per head of its population than any other country. Every year, about 250,000 immigrants settle in Canada—that is, one new arrival for every 12 people already living there. Canada also has 34 large ethnic groups (of more than 100,000 each) and many smaller ones.

Here is a 2006 article from "Open Immigration," a website run by *Capitalism* magazine. Do you agree with the writer's views?

Open Immigration: The Benefits Are Great. The Right Is Unquestionable. So Let Them Come.

Entry into the U.S. should be free for any foreigner, with the exception of criminals, would-be terrorists, and those carrying infectious diseases.

An end to immigration **quotas** is demanded by the principle of individual rights. Everyone has rights as an individual, not as a member of this or that nation. One has rights not by virtue of being American, but by virtue of being human. One doesn't have to be a resident of any particular country to have a moral entitlement to be secure from governmental coercion against one's life, liberty, and property.

In the words of the Declaration of Independence, government is instituted "to secure these rights"—to protect them against their violation by force or fraud.

A foreigner has rights just as much as an American. To be a foreigner is not to be a criminal.

[www.capmag.com]

> *Open borders*

There are many unmanned crossings on the long border between the United States and Canada.

> *School debate*

This school debate has teams of three on each side.

How to organize your own debate

How much should immigration be restricted? Have you formed your own opinion yet? You should now plan to explain your views to other people and persuade them that you are right. The best way to do this is to organize a debate with your classmates.

What kind of debate?

An organized debate is the best kind. If a crowd of students gets together and starts arguing, you will most likely end up with a shouting match. You will not learn anything from that. Your debate has to have two equal sides. It also has to have rules and a structure that everybody agrees to.

There are many debate formats to choose from. The simplest of all is a classroom debate, in which every student gets a chance to argue his or her opinion. However, a formal debate is a lot more rewarding, even if it is more complex to set up. In this, you start with a **motion** (a question or a statement) to argue about. A specially chosen panel of speakers (usually three people each in two teams) represents each side of the argument.

Who takes part?

The essential ingredient for a debate is opposing viewpoints. It is important to present different views on the topic being discussed, so that the audience members are likely to hear something that challenges or appeals to them. Make sure you have found people to present both positions. One side argues in favor of a topic (this is called the **proposition**). The other side argues against the case made by the first speaker (this is called the **opposition**).

How long will it last?

Set a time limit for the whole debate. If possible, keep the total running time to no more than an hour. You should also set time limits for each of the speakers (no longer than five minutes). This will leave roughly 30 minutes for questions from the audience and for voting at the end.

Who is in charge?

Choose someone to be the **moderator** (referee). The moderator does not take part in the debate but rather directs it, introducing the topic and keeping control of the speakers. Nobody may speak unless the moderator permits. A good moderator should treat both sides equally.

What happens?

The moderator explains the motion and the topic for debate. Then, the speakers on the panel take turns to read their prepared speeches. After this, the moderator asks the audience to pose questions to the speakers. The debate ends with short closing statements from both sides, restating their opinions with strong supporting evidence. Then, the audience votes, either for or against the motion. The moderator counts the votes and announces the winner.

 Debater's checklist

Remember to:

✔ research your subject thoroughly
✔ collect plenty of facts and evidence
✔ concentrate on the strongest points in your argument
✔ speak clearly and loudly enough for the audience to hear
✔ listen carefully to what other debaters say
✔ allow time for other people to express their opinions
✔ make notes of the weak points in your opponent's speech

Conclusion, for and against

Here is a quick survey of reasons why immigration takes place, and some of the main arguments for and against further restricting immigration.

Pushes and pulls

Humans have migrated across the world for millions of years. Almost every person in every land is descended from an immigrant. But what makes people want to move in the first place? There are two main factors—"push" and "pull." The "push" factors—such as war, poverty, disease, and natural disaster—drive people out of their homelands. The "pull" factors—safety, more jobs opportunities, better pay, and better education—attract them to other countries.

Pluses and minuses

Are immigrants good or bad for a country? Many people think they bring plenty of benefits to their new home. They may increase its wealth, take on jobs that others ignore, and improve businesses by lowering labor costs. On top of this, their culture may enrich and refresh society. Others believe immigrants may bring harm to a country. They may take jobs from native-born citizens, cause overcrowding, and overburden health and education services. Their cultural differences may increase divisions in society.

Refugees and asylum seekers

Thousands of people migrate because they are in fear of their lives. They flee from bloody wars and from government persecution. Many refugees ask for asylum—a safe place where they will be protected from arrest or ill-treatment by their own government. Sometimes they pay "people-smugglers" to transport them illegally across state borders. Should more wealthy and peaceful states welcome these refugees?

Drains and gains

Immigration frequently causes harm to the country that is left behind. Large numbers of highly trained professionals, such as doctors, nurses, and teachers, are migrating to wealthier states where they find better pay and career opportunities. This is a huge loss for their original homeland, which gave them their education. It is called the "brain drain." The destination countries enjoy a "brain gain." Can this problem be solved?

> *What do you think?*

> **This cartoon is called "Mixed Message." It was drawn by Nick Anderson of the Texas newspaper the *Houston Chronicle*. The "mixed message" it portrays is the conflict between the U.S. government's position of doing all it can to control illegal immigration and the employers' stance of wanting plentiful and cheap labor.**

What do you think now?

Did you have a definite opinion about immigration when you started this book? Or had you never really thought about the subject before? This book is not aimed at persuading you to take a view one way or another. Its object is to show you both sides of the debate and give you tips on how to think critically, how to find and look at evidence, and how to put your case effectively. So, what do you think—how much should immigration be restricted?

Find Out More

Projects

Are you descended from immigrants? Dig back into the roots of your own family. Ask older relatives about their ancestors, look into local records, and consult books and websites on genealogy (see below).

Do you want to emigrate? Ask your family and schoolmates if they would ever think of moving to another country. What are their reasons? Where would they go?

Make a list of famous and successful people in your country—politicians, musicians, athletes, artists, scientists. Find out how many of them are first- or second-generation immigrants.

Books

About immigration in general

Collier, Christopher, and James Lincoln Collier. *A Century of Immigration: 1820–1924*. New York: Benchmark, 2000.

Daniels, Roger. *American Immigration: A Student Companion*. New York: Oxford University Press, 2001.

Gelletly, LeeAnne. *The Changing Face of North America: Mexican Immigration*. Philadelphia: Mason Crest, 2004.

Legrain, Philippe. *Immigrants: Your Country Needs Them*. Princeton, N.J.: Princeton University Press, 2007.

Sources of evidence

Dudley, William. *Illegal Immigration: Examining Issues Through Political Cartoons*. Minneapolis: Tandem Library, 2003.

Houle, Michelle E. (ed.). *Immigration: Great Speeches in History*. Farmington Hills, Mich.: Greenhaven, 2004.

Refugees

Jolie, Angelina. *Notes from My Travels*: *Visits with Refugees in Africa, Cambodia, Pakistan and Ecuador*. New York: Simon & Schuster, 2003.

Moorehead, Caroline. *Human Cargo: A Journey Among Refugees*. New York: H. Holt, 2005.

Websites

Finding out about your ethnic background

www.pbs.org/wnet/aalives
Site of the movie *African American Lives* (2006), which tells migrants' stories

www.rootsforreal.com
Full of information and tips about tracing your ancestors

All sides of the debate

www.minutemanhq.com
A group campaigning for much stricter controls on immigration

www.openimmigration.com
Campaigning for free access for immigrants

Glossary

academic	from a higher school or university level
bias	in favor of one particular view or argument
detention camp	place where refugees and other immigrants are held before they are allowed to live freely in a country
detrimental	causing damage or harm to something
DNA	(short for deoxyribonucleic acid) chemical in all living things that passes on information about an individual's genetic makeup
drone	pilotless aircraft that is remotely controlled
economy	managing of money and other resources of a country, community, or business
emigrant	person who leaves his or her homeland and moves abroad
fundamentalist	someone who believes very strongly that the basic principles of his or her religious faith are literally true and unchangeable
gangmaster	person who employs a "gang" of illegal immigrants, who often work for little pay in harsh conditions
genetics	study of inherited traits and characteristics in humans
immigrant	person who enters a foreign country, having left his or her own country
Industrial Revolution	name given to the period since about 1700, during which the development of new machines and production methods has caused enormous changes throughout the world
infrastructure	basic facilities and systems (such as roads, railroads, and water supplies) that a country needs to run smoothly
maritime	near the sea, or concerned with ships and the sea
migrant	person who moves from one region or country to another
moderator	person who presides over a meeting or assembly; also known as a referee

motion	formal proposal or statement that forms the basis of a debate
opposition	case made by a speaker who is against (or disagrees with) a motion
oppression	using violence or unjust methods to persecute someone or keep the person under one's control
persecution	treating someone harshly or punishing someone for his or her political or religious beliefs
professional	belonging to an occupation that requires a long training period and special qualifications (such as a lawyer, a doctor, or a teacher)
proposition	case made by a speaker who is in favor of (or agrees with) a motion
quota	stated number of foreign people that will be accepted by a country
radar	method of detecting objects by measuring how they reflect radio waves
repression	keeping people firmly, even cruelly, under control
retina	delicate layer that lines the inner part of the eye and sends messages to the brain
sensor	device (often electronic) that detects sound or movement
Soviet Union	also called USSR. This was a communist empire centered on Russia that lasted from 1922 to 1991.
statistics	collection, organization, and interpretation of figures and other information
surveillance	close observation of a person or group under suspicion
Taliban	Islamic fundamentalist movement that ruled Afghanistan from 1996 to 2001
violation	breaking of a law, or the injuring of people or property
workforce	all the workers who are available in one country or project

Index